MW01233255

THE LORD'S PRAYER:

The Foundation of Prayer

Pastor Mark Amoateng, MD

ISBN # 13:
9781796378092

Copyright © 2019 Pastor Mark Amoateng, MD
All rights reserved. This book or any portion thereof may
not be reproduced or used in any manner whatsoever
without the express written permission of the publisher.

Published by
Advantage Publishing Group
www.publishingadvantagegroup.com

Contents

INTRODUCTION

One of the greatest things you can ever do is to pray. If there is only one thing you have to choose to occupy yourself with, choose prayer. Prayer is the Christian's greatest assignment. Prayer is what stirs and moves heaven and causes heaven to act and move on behalf of man. All the counsels and agenda of God run on prayer. Without prayer soul winning efforts will be futile. Without prayer preaching is impotent. Prayer is the fuel by which divinity moves. Prayer is the wheels on which divinity advances. And heaven cannot function on the earth without prayer.

Prayer is one of the most engaged in activities in Christianity. Many people pray. Some pray a lot and others do just enough to get by. Some of the people who pray hardly ever seem to get answers

1

to their prayers. Unanswered prayers have become the worry of many believers. And when prayers are not answered many people tend to blame God for failing to grant their request. But most of the time, if not all the time the problem is never God. God is not the reason why prayers are not answered. God is faithful. And whatever He says, He does. And He has promised to answer our prayers. When you call unto Him, He answers.

***"Call unto me, and I will answer thee…."
(Jeremiah 33:3 KJV)***

But there are many times you seemed to have called and there was no answer. There are several reasons why prayers are not answered. An accurate understanding of prayer I believe is one of the main reasons why many peoples prayers seem to be ineffective and inefficient. Why do we pray and how should we pray? What is the purpose of prayer? Till we get a very clear perspective of prayer it will remain a mystery. In this volume, you will have a clearer understanding of the foundations of prayer.

CHAPTER 1

CONCEPTS OF PRAYER

Prayer is an Invitation to God

In prayer, man invites God into the affairs of the earth. That is one of the great purposes of prayer. Till God is invited He does not intrude in your affairs against your will. Till you invite Him, He cannot come even if He wanted to. Not that He will not come. He cannot come not because He is weaker than man and cannot get His way with man. He cannot come because He cannot go against His own Word. His own Word is a Law unto Him. That reveals His faithfulness to us.

Why does God need an invitation into the affairs of the earth? Because God has given the earth to man. The earth belongs to man now. He received it from God.

"The heaven, [even] the heavens, [are] the LORD'S: but the earth hath he given to the children of men" (Psalms 115:16 KJV)

God has given the earth to the children of men. For God to intervene in the affairs of men, He needs man's invitation and prayer is that invitation.

For instance, when you rent a house or an apartment, the moment you sign the lease, get your keys and becomes the legal occupant, the landlord cannot enter the building anytime he or she wants. The house owner will need permission to come to your bedroom. If anything goes wrong in the building you will have to send a message to the property owner and then he or she comes in to fix it.

That is the same case with the earth. Man has the lease on the planet. He was given the dominion and the rulership to the earth. Man is in charge of this jurisdiction. God is the owner, man has the dominion on the planet. And God gave it over to

Him. Adam the first man became His vice-regent. God gave the earth to man at the very dawn of creation.

"So God created man in his [own] image, in the image of God created he him; male and female created he them. And God blessed them, and God said unto them, Be fruitful, and multiply, and replenish the earth, and subdue it: and have dominion over the fish of the sea, and over the fowl of the air, and over every living thing that moveth upon the earth" (Genesis 1:27:28 KJV)

When there is a problem on the earth, Man will have to invite God before He can manifest here and fix it in the same way the tenant must give permission to the property owner before he or she can access the bedroom. And the means of inviting God is called prayer.

Prayer is the operation of God on the earth.

On this earth, every being needs a body to function and operate here with fully. That is why human beings have bodies. The day a body ceases to function, on earth a person is declared dead. A spirit cannot function on the earth without a body. God too being a spirit needs to function on the earth through a body. When the Word which was God (being spirit), was manifesting in the world as Jesus, a body was prepared for Him.

"Wherefore when he cometh into the world, he saith, Sacrifice and offering thou wouldest not, but a body hast thou prepared me:" (Hebrews 10:5 KJV)

Jesus needed a body to function and operate fully on the earth. But when Jesus ascended to heaven, God then needed another body to operate and function through. So, God created the Church. The church is the body of Christ.

"And hath put all [things] under his feet, and gave him [to be] the head over all [things] to the church, Which is his body, the fulness of him that filleth all in all" (Ephesians 1:22-23 KJV)

The church which is the body of all born-again believer is the body of Christ. The operation and the functioning of God through the Church (Body of Christ) is called Prayer.

The primary goal of the church is to invite God and allow God to operate through it unhindered. God needs two things to establish His purposes and counsels on the earth: He needs a body and an invitation. God has provided Himself a body- the BODY OF CHRIST (which is the church). Now it is the church's responsibility to invite Him into the affairs of the earth.

The church which is the house of God is primarily the house of prayer.

"And said unto them, It is written, My house shall be called the house of prayer;..." **(Matthew 21:13 KJV)**

The body of Christ must now yield to the operation of the Christ within. And the more yielded the church is, the more prayer is offered. The yielded vessels of God are marked by much prayer.

Prayer is your contribution into the realm of the spirit

God made one universe which has two realms or dimensions- The Spiritual and the Physical. And there are beings living in each realm. There are activities in the spiritual realm in the same way as there are activities in the physical realm. And the truth of the matter is that the Spiritual realm controls the physical world. The activities of the spiritual realm determine and can manipulate the activities of the physical world.

Now man was made by God to have influence and live in the two realms. This is because man has three components; a spirit, soul, and body.

"And the very God of peace sanctify you wholly; and [I pray God] your whole spirit and soul and body be preserved blameless unto the coming of our Lord Jesus Christ" (1 Thessalonians 5:23 KJV)

With your spirit you make contact and deal in the spiritual realm and with your body, you make contact and deal in the physical world.

The great truth which you must realize is that the spiritual realm controls the happenings of the physical realm. The physical realm can be manipulated from the spiritual realm. The people who are able to make input and contribute to the spiritual realm are those who determine the happenings in the physical realm.

And as a Christian, the way to contribute and make inputs into the realm of the spirit is through prayer. Prayer is your contribution to the realm of the spirit. Anytime you pray you are exerting your influence and power in the realm of the spirit to determine the happenings in the physical world. And the reverse is also true when you don't pray someone else determines who happens around you.

Prayer is engaging Divinity.

Prayer has been defined as a communication between God and man. This definition is very true but brings a limitation to all the activities of prayer. There are sometimes in prayer you will talk, fellowship and communicate directly to God. But there are others times you are not speaking to God directly, but you might be speaking to the circumstances and the events of your life. You might even be speaking to cities, nations and inanimate things. And yet they are all forms of prayer.

So, then an all-encompassing definition of prayer is necessary. Prayer is actually engaging Divinity.

When in prayer, you talk directly to God, you are engaging divinity. And when in prayer you speak to the circumstances of your life by the power of God you are also engaging the divinity in you to overpower and overcome in life.

For example, the Bible declares that Elijah prayed that it should not rain.

"Elijah was a man just like us. He prayed earnestly that it would not rain, and it did not rain on the land for three and a half years" (James 5:17 NIV)

But when we go the book of first Kings and we

examine the prayer Elijah prayed, we realize that he didn't talk directly to God but rather he used God's power available to him (which is Divinity) and made a declaration which was fulfilled.

"And Elijah the Tishbite, [who was] of the inhabitants of Gilead, said unto Ahab, [As] the LORD God of Israel liveth, before whom I stand, there shall not be dew nor rain these years, but according to my word" (1 Kings 17:1 KJV)

Beloved, in prayer you engage Divinity whether directly in fellowship with the Father or by the Holy Spirit power and ability in you to change and transform situations. That was exactly what Peter, the apostle did. When he met the crippled man sitting by the beautiful gate, he did not speak to God directly, but by the ability of the Holy Spirit spoke to the crippled man. And that one too is prayer.

"Then Peter said, Silver and gold have I none; but such as I have give I thee: In the name of Jesus Christ of Nazareth rise up and walk" (Acts 3:6 KJV)

The Lord's Prayer

CHAPTER 2

THE LORD'S PRAYER -
A TEACHING ON PRAYER

Our Father, which art in heaven,

Hallowed be thy Name.

Thy Kingdom come. Thy will be done on earth,

As it is in heaven.

Give us this day our daily bread.

And forgive us our trespasses,

As we forgive them that trespass against us.

And lead us not into temptation,

But deliver us from evil.

For thine is the kingdom,

The power, and the glory, Forever and ever.

Amen.

The above prayer is popularly known as the Lord's Prayer. It is recited by many people and churches all across the globe. Many people have received help and edification by reciting it.

These precious words which have become a recital were first uttered by the Lord Jesus Christ, hence the name THE LORD'S PRAYER.

But a careful study of the scriptures will reveal that the Lord's prayer was not just meant to be a recital. It is supposed to be more than a recital. Actually, it was an answer to a question asked by one of Jesus' disciple. Let's examine the scripture.

"And it came to pass, that, as he was praying in a certain place, when he ceased, one of his disciples said unto him, Lord, teach us to pray, as John also taught his disciples. And he said unto them, When ye pray, say, Our Father which art in heaven, Hallowed be thy name. Thy kingdom come. Thy will be done, as in heaven, so in earth. Give us day by day

our daily bread. And forgive us our sins; for we also forgive every one that is indebted to us. And lead us not into temptation; but deliver us from evil" (Luke 11:1-4 KJV)

From the above portion of scripture, we realize that the Lord's prayer was teaching on prayer Jesus gave to His disciples. Jesus was asked to teach on prayer and the teaching He gave on prayer is what is now called The Lord's Prayer. So actually, the Lord's prayer is more than a recital; it is a teaching on prayer. Secrets and great lessons on prayer are hidden in those few lines. Jesus did more than give the church a recital to repeat to God. He gave us the foundations and basis of effective praying. The secrets to answered prayers are revealed to us.

In this book, we will explore the riches of the lessons on prayer as communicated by Jesus.

HALLOWED BE THY NAME

"And he said unto them, When ye pray, say, Our Father which art in heaven, Hallowed be

thy name" (Luke 11:1 KJV)

The first foundation of prayer is giving attention to the name of the father. The Heavenly Father is the first subject you address in prayer. And what about the Father do you address? His name! *Hallowed be thy name!*

If the goal of your prayer is for the name of the Lord to be hallowed, then your prayer will be answered hundred percent of the time. If the purpose of your prayer is to glorify the name of the Lord; if the purpose of your prayers is to honor His name, you will not have to beg Him to answer them. Actually, before you call, He will answer. *"And it shall come to pass, that before they call, I will answer; and while they are yet speaking, I will hear" (Isaiah 65:24 KJV).* The greatest thing on your mind when you pray must be the name of the Lord and not your desires.

The name of the Lord according to the scriptures connotes His glory. You cannot separate the name of the Lord from His glory. Anytime the Lord's name is mentioned His glory is implied. *"I [am] the LORD: that [is] my name: and my glory*

will I not give to another, neither my praise to graven images" (Isaiah 42:8 KJV)

Again, in the book of Exodus, Moses, the Man of God demanded to see the glory of God and God told Moses that He will proclaim His name to Moses. Which means the name of the Lord equates His glory. **"And he said, I beseech thee, shew me thy glory. And he said, I will make all my goodness pass before thee, and I will proclaim the name of the LORD before thee; and will be gracious to whom I will be gracious, and will shew mercy on whom I will shew mercy" (Exodus 33:18-19 KJV)**

The name of the Lord is His glory. And the glory of the Lord denotes His very Essence or Substance.

When you are praying and the basis of your prayer is the hallowing of His name, what you are actually saying is that His glory should be revealed or His essence be manifested. When you say *'hallowed be thy name'*, what you are actually saying is that God let your glory manifest. You are saying receive the honor. You are declaring God reveal who you are.

17

"…. Like this: Our Father in heaven, Reveal, who you are" (Matthew 6:9 MSG)

And because He wants His glory and has no plans of sharing His glory with no other, He will answer. God will do anything for His name. *"I [am] the LORD: that [is] my name: and my glory will I not give to another, neither my praise to graven images" (Isaiah 42:8 KJV).* Any prayer with the purpose of manifesting the glory of God will be answered with speed.

One of the greatest and awes-trucking miracles we read about in the bible is the dividing of the Red Sea. Now that happened in response to a prayer geared at the glory of the Lord. It was an answer that brought honor to the name of the Lord. *"I will harden the hearts of the Egyptians so that they will go in after them. And I will gain glory through Pharaoh and all his army, through his chariots and his horsemen. The Egyptians will know that I am the LORD when I gain glory through Pharaoh, his chariots and his horsemen" (Exodus 14:17 NIV)*

The reason why God divided the red sea was not

just so that the Israelites would pass through on dry ground. Of course, they wanted to cross to the other side. But there was a higher purpose and reason that moved God. And that purpose was the hallowing of his name and His glory. The need was that they cross the Red Sea. That was the need. But God didn't do it because of the need. He did it because of His glory.

For instance, you may need ten thousand dollars to accomplish a task. You must get it for a particular purchase or acquisition. If you want a quick response don't pray just because of the need, pray for the glory God would get when that need is met. When you pray because of His glory, the need will be met. That is the meaning of 'hallowed be your name".

That was how they prayed in Bible times and they got bible results. What God desires is that He doesn't want anything to tamper with His name. **"A [good] name [is] rather to be chosen than great riches,..." (Proverbs 22;1 KJV).** This verse is true, not only for man but for any being in the universe- and that includes God. This is because God and His word are one.

In the corporate or business world the name of a company reflects the glory of the company. That is how come all companies ensure excellent and good customer service so that their reputation which their name is not messed up. For if you mess up your name, you are messing up your brand.

In the same vein, God does not want to pollute His name, because His name speaks of His glory.

God acts in such a way that His name will be honored and hallowed.

In the book Ezekiel, God declared that He brought the Israelites out of Egypt so that His name will be honored rather than be polluted or profaned.

"But for the sake of my name I did what would keep it from being profaned in the eyes of the nations they lived among and in whose sight I had revealed myself to the Israelites by bringing them out of Egypt" (Ezekiel 20:9 NIV)

The greatest reason you can get God to act is for

His own namesake. He will do anything when His name is hallowed. You might be in need of a miracle, a financial breakthrough or a favor. Or you simply need a change of circumstances. You must just make your demands and tie them to His glory; He will act swiftly on your behalf.

Jesus, who was the Word from the beginning has been with the Father in heaven for an eternity before He came down to the earth. He discovered one thing about the Father, that He would not allow His name to be polluted or profaned ever. He would not let any man or thing pollute His name. And I believe Jesus noticed that if any person comes in prayer who is interested in the preservation and hallowing of the name of His Father, he will get the quick and prompt response from the Father. The father will tell the angels this person came to hallow my name, what can we do so that my name is hallowed or venerated?

Now this point about the name of God becomes very crucial when you want the anger or judgment of God against a person, a city or even a nation averted. God will defer His anger for His name sake.

"For my name's sake will I defer mine anger, and for my praise will I refrain for thee, that I cut thee not off" (Isaiah 48:9 KJV)

For example, if there is a plague of death or destruction against a family, and you go to God in prayer declaring, 'God please change it, the famine is very bad, the people are very sick and hungry, God please look on their miserable faces and do something.' That is praying an emotional prayer. It might get results and it might not also get results. But if you will pray based on His word and say, 'Heavenly Father, show us mercy, heal our land, provide for us, avert the plague for your name sake', you are sure to get speedy attention from the throne of grace. God is a great God and a mighty one.

Your title or position cannot move Him, because He is the greatest and the strongest. You can get much from Him when you pray like, 'Father, I am the pastor of this church please save my children, or I am the president of this nation bless us'. But you are certainly going to get a response when you pray like this,' Father, for your name sake, bless our nation, for your name sake save our children"

God will never give His glory away. And the way His glory goes to another is by polluting it. Let's examine this in Isaiah 48:11;

"For mine own sake, [even] for mine own sake, will I do [it]: for how should [my name] be polluted? and I will not give my glory unto another" (Isaiah 48:11 KJV)

God will answer you for His own name sake. This means He will do this to prove Himself that He alone is God. He would not do it because you are such a kind person or a good woman or man. His essence or name overrides any other reason no matter how true it is. The surest foundation Jesus gave to us for prayer is Hallowed be your name!

HOW DAVID PRAYED ACCORDING TO THE NAME OF THE LORD

King David was such an amazing man who walked with God and knew how to pray to get answers. He understood the hallowing of God's name and used it in His prayers. Let's examine a few.

When David wanted God to forgive him his iniquities, he did not go to God to bargain because he was a king or even the man after the heart of God. He asked God to forgive him for God's own name sake.

"For thy name's sake, O LORD, pardon mine iniquity; for it [is] great" (Psalms 25:11 KJV)

David knew how great his sin was. He knew he had disappointed God but he also knew God will do anything for His name sake and so he went to God on that ticket.

When David needed God to lead and guide him in the affairs of his life, that is exactly how he prayed too.

"For thou [art] my rock and my fortress; therefore for thy name's sake lead me, and guide me" (Psalms 31:3 KJV)

David later realized that he was led for the sake of God's name and not for his own efforts or goodness. He declares in the twenty-third Psalm:

"He restoreth my soul: he leadeth me in the

paths of righteousness for his name's sake"
(Psalms 23:3 KJV)

You must pray like David. Lead me in the paths of prosperity, peace, abundance, for your name sake oh God! Lead me into a good job, a good marriage for your name sake. When you do, you will be hallowing the Father's name in your prayers.

Look at other times King David prayed and he made reference to the name of the Lord.

"Help us, O God of our salvation, for the glory of thy name: and deliver us, and purge away our sins, for thy name's sake" (Psalms 79:9 KJV)

"But do thou for me, O GOD the Lord, for thy name's sake: because thy mercy [is] good, deliver thou me" (Psalms 109:21 KJV)

"Quicken me, O LORD, for thy name's sake: for thy righteousness' sake bring my soul out of trouble" (Psalms 143:11 KJV)

"Not unto us, O LORD, not unto us, but unto thy name give glory, for thy mercy, [and] for thy truth's sake" (Psalms 115:1 KJV)

Not only David prayed that way. The prophets of old also prayed the same way. When they prayed, they believed for an answer because of God's name.

Look at how Jeremiah prayed:

"O LORD, though our iniquities testify against us, do thou [it] for thy name's sake: for our backslidings are many; we have sinned against thee" (Jeremiah 14:7 KJV)

And again in the same chapter:

"Do not abhor [us], for thy name's sake, do not disgrace the throne of thy glory: remember, break not thy covenant with us" (Jeremiah 14:21 KJV)

Prophet Daniel also prayed likewise:

"O Lord, hear; O Lord, forgive; O Lord, hearken and do; defer not, for thine own sake,

O my God: for thy city and thy people are called by thy name" (Daniel 9:19 KJV)

Daniel said God hear and grant my request for your own sake, because your people are called by your name. Daniel in another way was telling God your name is at stake.

WHY WE PRAY IN THE NAME OF JESUS?

Now, this is one of the main reasons why we pray in the name of Jesus. The name of Jesus is not a punctuation mark we use at the end of a prayer. You must use the Name of Jesus with this revelation in mind. You must not use it religiously. Actually, before Jesus left, He told us to pray in His name.

"And whatsoever ye shall ask in my name, that will I do, that the Father may be glorified in the Son. If ye shall ask any thing in my name, I will do [it]" (John 14:13-14 KJV)

There is a reason why He gave us the authority and the right to pray in His name. The reason is that the Name, Jesus is the hallowed name of the

Godhead. The whole of the Godhead has their expression in Jesus.

"For in him dwelleth all the fulness of the Godhead bodily" (Colossians 2:9 KJV)

So, when the name, Jesus is mentioned, the Father is invoked, the Son is invoked and the Holy Spirit too is invoked. And the name of Jesus was hallowed because of His sacrificial death on the cross of Calvary.

"Let this mind be in you, which was also in Christ Jesus: Who, being in the form of God, thought it not robbery to be equal with God: But made himself of no reputation, and took upon him the form of a servant, and was made in the likeness of men: And being found in fashion as a man, he humbled himself, and became obedient unto death, even the death of the cross. <u>Wherefore God also hath highly exalted him, and given him a name which is above every name: That at the name of Jesus every knee should bow,</u> of [things] in heaven, and [things] in earth, and [things] under the earth; And [that] every tongue should confess

that Jesus Christ [is] Lord, to the glory of God the Father" (Philippians 2:5-11 KJV)

Now you know that the name of Jesus is not a cliché or a just a theological way to end pray. But when you pray in the name of Jesus you are invoking the already hallowed name of the Godhead.

The Apostle Peter had this revelation when he prayed for the man who sat at the temple gate called Beautiful.

"Then Peter said, Silver and gold have I none; but such as I have give I thee: In the name of Jesus Christ of Nazareth rise up and walk" (Acts 3:6 KJV)

And God will always respond to His hallowed name and act for His own name sake.

And now you know the first foundation of prayer, which is the hallowing of the Father's name. You just don't have to say it with your mouth but more importantly, pray in consciousness and revelation of this blessed truth. If you will walk in this consciousness and understanding from today, you will have more prayers answered than before.

"Now that you know these things, you will be blessed if you do them" (John 13:17 NIV)

CHAPTER 3

THY KINGDOM COME –
THY WILL BE DONE

In this chapter, we turn our attention to the second foundation of prayer. The second issue you address in prayer is the Kingdom of God.

"Thy kingdom come. Thy will be done in earth, as [it is] in heaven" (Matthew 6:9 KJV)

Now note that when the will of God is established on the earth, His Kingdom has come. The coming of His Kingdom is His will.

God wants the establishment of His Kingdom more than anything else. If you will concern yourself with what God is concerned with, you will have your needs and wants met without asking. The most important thing to God is His kingdom. If you will pray Kingdom advancement prayers and work to advance His kingdom, your needs will vanish as if they never existed.

"But seek ye first the kingdom of God, and his righteousness; and all these things shall be added unto you" (Matthew 6:33 KJV)

The chiefest and the first thing to pray and seek for in prayer is the Kingdom of God. If you will do this, the things you are begging God for, worried about and losing sleep on will be added to you effortlessly.

Many people spend hours praying and hardly will they pray concerning the interest of God's Kingdom. One of the means to have quick answers is asking the Kingdom of God to manifest on the earth. You pray for the Kingdom to rule your city, nation, or neighborhood. You pray for the Kingdom of God to be established in the hearts of men. You pray for souls to be saved. You pray for churches to grow and ministries to flourish. If this becomes your first point of call in prayer you come to belong to the class of people who receives answers to their prayers before they actually upon God.

"And it shall come to pass, that before they call, I will answer; and while they are yet speaking, I will hear" (Isaiah 65:24 KJV)

Beloved, I want to ask you when did you last fast just that Jesus will reign in your city? When did you go on a 3 -day fast and your goal was not to pray for your special need or that you had a bad dream, but your aim was to see the move of God in your family, school or workplace? Our prayers should sound something like this; 'Heavenly Father, I declare that the spread of your Kingdom will know no end. Your glory shall know no bounds. Your righteousness rules in the nations of the world. Oh Lord God! rule in the courthouses, rule in the hospitals, rule in our schools. Let your righteousness be revealed. Let souls be saved in our cities in large numbers. Let there be a strong move of your Spirit in our churches.' This is a prayer saying essentially, let your Kingdom come.

If you concern yourself with such matters, God will concern Himself with your needs and add them unto you.

The most precious possession of God is His Kingdom. Let me give you an idea what the Kingdom of God is really about. God's Kingdom has been His main agenda since creation.

In the book of Genesis when God declared that He wanted to make man in His image and likeness so that man would have dominion, He was referring to the establishment of His Kingdom on earth.

"And God said, Let us make man in our image, after our likeness: <u>and let them have dominion</u> over the fish of the sea, and over the fowl of the air, and over the cattle, and over all the earth, and over every creeping thing that creepeth upon the earth" (Genesis 1:26 KJV)

The word Kingdom simply means the Domain where the Dominion of the King is. When God gave the dominion to man, He was telling man to spread His Kingdom. Man's original mandate was the mandate of the Kingdom. The greatest message God sends a man to preach is the message of the Kingdom.

The first sermon Jesus preached was the message of the Kingdom of God.

"Now after that John was put in prison, Jesus came into Galilee, preaching the gospel of the kingdom of God, And saying, The time is fulfilled, and the kingdom of God is at hand: repent ye, and believe the gospel" (Mark 1:14-15 KJV)

Because Jesus knew the priority God gives to His Kingdom, He made it His first message. And actually, His last message just before His ascension too was about the Kingdom of God.

"To whom also he shewed himself alive after his passion by many infallible proofs, being seen of them forty days, <u>and speaking of the things pertaining to the kingdom of God</u>" (Acts 1:3 KJV)

That was how important the Kingdom message is to Jesus. And I believe because the disciples had also learned the preeminence of the Kingdom message, their last question to Jesus was about the Kingdom.

"When they therefore were come together, they asked of him, saying, Lord, wilt thou at this time restore again the kingdom to Israel? (Acts 1:6 KJV)

Friend, God is interested in His Kingdom. Let your prayer be Kingdom advancement prayers and you will be a marvel to your world. Let your prayer be; 'Thy Kingdom come'.

The apostles of the Lord Jesus Christ also preached about the Kingdom. For they also realized how important the Kingdom is to the heart of the Father.

Philip preached the Kingdom to the city of Samaria and there was a revival.

"But when they believed Philip <u>preaching the things concerning the kingdom of God,</u> and the name of Jesus Christ, they were baptized, both men and women" (Acts 8:12 KJV)

Paul, the apostle also preached the message of the Kingdom in his ministry.

"And when they had appointed him a day, there came many to him into [his] lodging; to whom <u>he expounded and testified the kingdom of God,</u> persuading them concerning Jesus, both out of the law of Moses, and [out of] the prophets, from morning till evening" (Acts 28:23 KJV)

The apostles expended their life, resources ,and energies on the Kingdom of God. We can't do anything less.

As a matter of fact, the very reason Jesus came into world was to get and obtain a Kingdom for the Father. How do we know? In one of His parables, Jesus spoke of this truth about Himself.

"He said therefore, A certain nobleman went into a far country to receive for himself a kingdom, and to return" (Luke 19:12 KJV)

Jesus is that nobleman who went into a far country to receive a Kingdom.

Again, the blessed Apostle expounds this truth further;

"Then [cometh] the end, <u>when he shall have delivered up the kingdom to God, even the Father;</u> when he shall have put down all rule and all authority and power" (1 Corinthians 15:24 KJV)

The Kingdom is the Father's desire and joy. And that is why Jesus was sent. How is this grandeur mission of Jesus unfolding?

"Far above all principality, and power, and might, and dominion, and every name that is named, not only in this world, but also in that which is to come: And hath put all [things] under his feet, and gave him [to be] the head over all [things] to the church, Which is his body, the fulness of him that filleth all in all" (Ephesians 1:21-23 KJV)

The above scripture explains to us how Jesus set out to obtain the Kingdom to God. When Jesus came into the world, He preached the Kingdom and then He died. When He died He rose again and ascended into heaven. He is seated and has all things under His feet now. And he is the head of the Church, which is His body. And this church which is His body is 'the fulness of Him that filleth all in all.' So, the first entity Jesus obtained after His ascension is the church. And the church is the initial seed of the Kingdom. And the expansion of the church is the expansion of God's Kingdom.

God's Kingdom is in full manifestation 'when God is all and in all.' Look at what Apostle Paul said in 1 Corinthians chapter fifteen.

"And when all things shall be subdued unto him, then shall the Son also himself be subject unto him that put all things under him, that God may be all in all" (1 Corinthians 15:28 KJV)

God wants to subdue all things under His feet. And that was His original dream in creating man. When He said let us make man in our image and likeness and let Him have dominion, He was actually saying that man must subdue all things under Him, God. Actually, God told man to subdue the earth.

"And God blessed them, and God said unto them, Be fruitful, and multiply, and replenish the earth, <u>and subdue it</u>: and have dominion over the fish of the sea, and over the fowl of the air, and over every living thing that moveth upon the earth"

To subdue means to make an object or a person express one's desire or will. So, the plan of God is for all things to be filled with Himself so that all things can express and manifest His desire and will. In creating man in His image and likeness, He was actually making man to look like Him and function like Him. So that if you met the man of God's dream, you couldn't distinguish between Him and God. God wants His creation to be exactly like Him in expression and function.

And when that is achieved, we can say God has become all and in all. And this is the Kingdom of God.

And the church is the initial seed of God becoming all and in all. How do we know?

Apostle Paul reveals that to us:

"And hath put all [things] under his feet, and gave him [to be] the head over all [things] to the church, Which is his body, the fulness of him that filleth all in all" (Ephesians 1:22-23 KJV)

The church is the firstfruit of the kingdom, and the plan of God is that the church will expand and become the kingdom. Beloved, we who are born again now, we are part of the initial plan of God and if we overcome, in the ages to come we will reign and rule with Him.

Dear Friend, let your prayer be Kingdom advancement prayers. Give towards the spread of the Kingdom of God. Seek first the Kingdom. Be interested in the growth of your church. Be involved in the winning of souls into the church. Find a need in God's house and meet it.

From today let your prayers be Kingdom first. Not your comfort first, or marriage first or your money first. But let your Kingdom come. If you pray concerning God's Kingdom which is the dearest thing on His heart, He will certainly add to you whatsoever you desire. Pray for the salvation of the souls. Pray for the influence of the body of Christ to increase and spread throughout the earth as the waters cover the sea.

"Thy kingdom come…." (Matthew 6:10 KJV)
Oh Lord Reign! Jesus REIGN, You are Judah's Lion, Reign.
From shore to shore, Jesus Reign.
From Coast to coast, Jesus Reign.
Wherever the Sun successive journeys run, Jesus Reign.
Till the Kingdoms of this world become the Kingdoms of our Lord and of His Christ, Jesus reign forever and ever!

CHAPTER 4

GIVE US, FORGIVE US, LEAD US AND DELIVER US!

In this chapter, we come to the next foundation of prayer. This time the prayer turns man-ward; that is to say, the needs of man are now addressed. The first portion of prayer must be Godward. Prayer must first of all be God-ward. *"Our Father which art in heaven, Hallowed be thy name. Thy kingdom come. Thy will be done in earth, as [it is] in heaven".* His name hallowed, His Kingdom desired and His Will established.

The purpose of prayer is to meet God's need first before your need. 'Hallowed be thy name"- that is a need of God. 'Thy Kingdom come' is a need of

God. 'Thy Will be done'- is a need of God. Then comes the need of men. In prayer, the heart and mind of man must tilt Godward first.

Prayer addresses four main needs of Man. These are:

1.GIVE US

2.FORGIVE US

3.LEAD US

4.DELIVER US

"<u>Give us</u> this day our daily bread. And <u>forgive us</u> our debts, as we forgive our debtors. And <u>lead us</u> not into temptation, but <u>deliver us</u> from evil..." (Matthew 6:11 KJV)

GIVE US

The first need of man that is addressed in prayer is today's needs. 'Give us this day our daily bread'. By prayer your everyday needs are satisfied. When the Bible talks about bread, it makes reference to your satisfaction and not bread specifically. Whatever you require to have a fulfilled day is included. This includes food, shelter, clothing, protection, safety, and companionship. God provides your physiological needs, Psychological needs, and self-fulfillment needs.

But God does not want us to worry about tomorrow and He asks us to request for today's bread. You ask for today's bread and you prophesy concerning tomorrow. You must trust God to meet all your daily needs. Man wants to be in charge, but God wants man to trust Him.

"Therefore I tell you, do not worry about your life, what you will eat or drink; or about your body, what you will wear. Is not life more important than food, and the body more important than clothes? Look at the birds of the air; they do not sow or reap or store away in barns, and yet your heavenly Father feeds them. Are you not much more valuable than they? Who of you by worrying can add a single hour to his life? "And why do you worry about clothes? See how the lilies of the field grow. They do not labor or spin. Yet I tell you that

not even Solomon in all his splendor was dressed like one of these. If that is how God clothes the grass of the field, which is here today and tomorrow is thrown into the fire, will he not much more clothe you, O you of little faith? So do not worry, saying, 'What shall we eat?' or 'What shall we drink?' or 'What shall we wear?" (Matthew 6:25-31 KJV)

God wants you to trust Him as your daily source. He is the supplier and the giver of everything good. Whatever we see as source physically is just a channel or a means to deliver to us our needs.

In the wilderness when the Israelites demanded bread, God gave them manna from above. God promised them that He will supply the manna daily, but they will not trust God's word. They were to come and gather just enough for each day. Instead, they will come out and gather for several days. Simply because they could not trust God.

"And Moses said, Let no man leave of it till the morning. Notwithstanding they hearkened not unto Moses; but some of them left of it until the morning, and it bred worms,

**and stank: and Moses was wroth with them"
(Exodus 16:19-20 KJV)**

FORGIVE US

*"And forgive us our debts, as we forgive our
debtors" (Matthew 6:12 KJV)*

Man needs forgiveness from sin. And prayer is a
means where forgiveness is received. In prayer
when we confess our sins God is faithful to
forgive us.

*"If we confess our sins, he is faithful and just
to forgive us [our] sins, and to cleanse us from
all unrighteousness" (1 John 1:9 KJV)*

He is faithful and just to forgive us because the
blood of Jesus which was shed on the cross of
Calvary and presented before the Mercy Seat has
the power to cleanse us from all sin. Hallelujah!

*"But if we walk in the light, as he is in the
light, we have fellowship one with another,
and the blood of Jesus Christ his Son*

cleanseth us from all sin" (1 John 1:7 KJV)

Beloved, anytime you sin you need to be conscious of the blood of Jesus to cleanse you. Why is this so? I will tell you. Sin is the strength of the devil. And sin is the sting of death.

"The sting of death [is] sin;..."(1 Corinthians 15:56 KJV)

The devil gets the legal grounds to attack a person because of sin. This is because sin can break the hedge of protection around an individual.

Listen to the counsel of Apostle Paul;

"Be ye angry, and sin not: let not the sun go down upon your wrath: Neither give place to the devil" (Ephesians 4:26-27 KJV)

When you get angry, you don't have to sin, because the sin gives the devil a foothold in your life. Let's read the same verse in the Amplified version:

"Leave no [such] room or foothold for the devil [give no opportunity to him]"

(Ephesians 4:27 AMP)

The devil looks for evidence or an opportunity to hurt you. Because he is the accuser of the brethren.

"And I heard a loud voice saying in heaven, Now is come salvation, and strength, and the kingdom of our God, and the power of his Christ: <u>for the accuser of our brethren is cast down</u>, which accused them before our God day and night" (Revelation 12:10 KJV)

In the book of Zechariah, satan stood to accuse Joshua the high priest because of his filthy garments which represent the stains of sin and iniquity. The filthy garments had to be removed so that the accuser would have no grounds to accuse him.

"And he shewed me Joshua the high priest standing before the angel of the LORD, and Satan standing at his right hand to resist him. And the LORD said unto Satan, The LORD rebuke thee, O Satan; even the LORD that hath chosen Jerusalem rebuke thee: [is] not

this a brand plucked out of the fire? Now Joshua was clothed with filthy garments, and stood before the angel. And he answered and spake unto those that stood before him, saying, Take away the filthy garments from him. And unto him he said, Behold, I have caused thine iniquity to pass from thee, and I will clothe thee with change of raiment" *(Zechariah 3:1-4 KJV)*

Now when you sin, you have an advocate with the Father, the Lord Jesus the righteous. Because of His blood, the devil has no grounds to accuse us before a holy God. Jesus Christ has fully settled forever all that a holy God could have against us, and it is paid in full. We are forgiven and justified. But in prayer, you receive what Jesus has already accomplished for you which is the forgiveness of sins and trespasses. And when your sins are forgiven, the devil has no foothold or evidence against you.

LEAD US

"And lead us not into temptation...." (Matthew 6:13 KJV)

One great need for every man is divine leading or direction. What a man will do? Where a man will stay? Who you will marry? Which type of investment to invest? And many other questions are all why a person needs divine guidance and leading from God. For a man to know his own way is not in himself.

"O LORD, I know that the way of man [is] not in himself: [it is] not in man that walketh to direct his steps" (Jeremiah 10:23 KJV)

But in prayer, we can receive divine directions and guidance. When you are led in this life your path becomes easy and your end is glorious. King David, prayed for divine direction multiple times.

"Lead me, O LORD, in thy righteousness because of mine enemies; make thy way straight before my face" (Psalms 5:8 KJV)

And again He asked for guidance in the name of

the Lord;

"For thou [art] my rock and my fortress; therefore for thy name's sake lead me, and guide me" (Psalms 31:3 KJV)

And God heard and answered him. He was led in paths of righteousness.

"...he leadeth me in the paths of righteousness for his name's sake" (Psalms 23:3 KJV)

To be led in the paths of righteousness means you are led in the right direction. The message Bible makes this point clearer.

"True to your word, you let me catch my breath and send me in the right direction" (Psalms 23:3 MSG)

So, in prayer, you can ask that God leads you in the right way to go and again you can ask specifically that you are not led into temptation. *'Lead us not into temptation..'*

The reason why you ask God not to lead you into

temptation is that the Lord knows how to deliver you out of temptations.

"The Lord knoweth how to deliver the godly out of temptations, *and to reserve the unjust unto the day of judgment to be punished..."* *(2 Peter 2:9 KJV)*

How does God deliver the godly out of temptations? He does it in two ways. Apostle Paul explains it to us:

"There hath no temptation taken you but such as is common to man: but God [is] faithful, who will not suffer you to be tempted above that ye are able; but will with the temptation also make a way to escape, that ye may be able to bear [it]" (1 Corinthians 10:13 KJV)

Firstly, God will make sure the temptation which comes your way is common to man. That is to say, the temptation is not beyond human experience. Don't let the devil make you feel special by tricking you to believe that your temptation is out of this world and that there is no help out of it.

Anytime you are faced with temptation tell yourself, 'this temptation is not special. People have overcome similar temptation and so I can also overcome it'. The moment you do this the temptation has lost its power over you. The scripture declares God is faithful He will not let you be tempted above that which you are able to bear.

Secondly, God will always provide a way of escape from any temptation. So, whenever there is a temptation confronting you, just know that there is certainly a way of escape out it. Your prayer then actually should be, 'Oh Lord show me the way of escape from this temptation'. Many times, people fall into temptation because they cannot locate the way out of the temptation.

But the reason why the devil will tempt anyone in the first place is so that the person can sin. And the moment you sin he has a foothold or evidence against you. For example, when Paul, the apostle said, ***"Be ye angry, and sin not: let not the sun go down upon your wrath." (Ephesians 4:26 KJV).*** What he was actually saying is that you have been led into temptation by been angry, but make sure you don't continue in the temptation to sin. You need to find the way of escape out of that temptation.

In prayer, you find grace and help not to sin, but even if you sin, He is faithful and just to forgive you.

DELIVER US

"....but deliver us from evil:..." (Matthew 6:13 KJV)

The last portion of prayer deals with the evil one and his evil. We should not spend all our prayer time praying about the devil. Jesus puts that at the last portion of prayer.

There are two evils you must be delivered from. The first one is the evil one-the devil. Read the prayer Jesus Himself prayed for His disciples before He left. He prayed that they will be delivered from the evil one.

"My prayer is not that you take them out of

the world but that you <u>protect them from the</u>
<u>evil one</u>" (John 17:15 NIV)

In prayer, you receive protection and preservation
from the devil and his cohorts, because *"For we*
wrestle not against flesh and blood, but
against principalities, against powers, against
the rulers of the darkness of this world,
against spiritual wickedness in high [places]"
(Ephesians 6:12 KJV)

The second evil you need to be delivered from is
Ignorance. Ignorance or the lack of knowledge is
the power of darkness. When you are in the dark
the evil one is empowered to destroy you.

"My people are destroyed for lack of
knowledge: because thou hast rejected
knowledge, I will also reject thee, that thou
shalt be no priest to me: seeing thou hast
forgotten the law of thy God, I will also forget
thy children" (Hosea 4:6 KJV)

In prayer, you ask God to deliver you from the
evil one and ignorance.

Lastly, if we will examine all the four ways Jesus shows us to pray concerning our needs, we will realize that prayer should not be selfish. Jesus says to pray this way; Give us, not give me; forgive us, not forgive me; lead us, not lead me; and finally deliver us, not deliver me.

We must learn to pray for the needs of others too. Pray for God's provision, guidance, protection, and love for all men.

CHAPTER 5

THE KINGDOM, THE POWER, AND THE GLORY

"…. For thine is the kingdom, and the power, and the glory, for ever. Amen" (Matthew 6:13 KJV)

Jesus gave the whole summary of the foundations of prayer in the very last portion as quoted in the verse above. All prayer concentrates on three attributes of God; His Kingdom, His power, and His Glory. Actually, Jesus could have said when you pray declare, 'for thine is the Kingdom, the power and the glory for ever Amen' and He would have included all the aspects in that short phrase.

HIS GLORY

The first part **'Our Father in Heaven, Hallowed be thy name'** refers to God's glory. The name of God refers to His Glory as explained in chapter two.

HIS KINGDOM

The second part talks directly about God's Kingdom; **'Thy kingdom come. Thy will be done in earth, as [it is] in heaven'.** The coming of God's Kingdom is the manifestation of His will on the earth as it is in Heaven.

HIS POWER

Now all the other parts are met and supplied by God's power.

1. Give us this day our daily bread -That is met by God's power.
2. Forgive us our debts- is met by the power of the blood of Jesus and the power of His Love.

3. Lead us not into temptation- is answered by the power of His wisdom.
4. Deliver us -is answered by His power to protect and preserve.

Beloved, in conclusion, prayer, implores upon the Glory of God and His power and long for the establishment of His Kingdom.

ABOUT THE AUTHOR

Dr. Mark K. Amoateng, is the founder and Senior Pastor of Christ Palace International Ministries and President of Mark Amoateng Ministries. He is a unique and vibrant minister of God for these present times. He ministers under the divine influence of the Holy Spirit and strong insight in the Word of God. Dr. Mark is an awesome teacher of the Word of God. His messages are so profound and yet have a touch of simplicity.

Pastor Mark's faith is contagious and affects those who come into contact with him. He picks the Word of God and holds it as it is. His operation in the prophetic, combined with his faith and insight in the Word of God, makes his impact strong, effective and long lasting. Give him a little attention and the divine verities of the

61

Word of God become real to you.

Pastor Mark is a medical doctor by training but now pursues the high calling of God on his life fulltime. He is happily married to Lady Pastor Magdelene Doris Amoateng also a medical doctor by profession. Their marriage is graciously blessed with two children, Amethyst and Johanan. Together, they fulfill the glorious divine mandate on their lives. He lives in Houston, Texas with his family. He is the author of a few titles including How to receive from God and The Wonders of Speaking in tongues. He also authors the highly anointed daily devotionals called The Voice Devotional.

CONTACT US

Website: www.MarkAmoateng.net

Email address:markamoateng6@gmail.com

Mailing Address:
Mark Amoateng Ministries
21821 Katy Fwy 102C, PMB 185
Katy, TX 77450

Whenever you visit Houston or if you live in the Houston area, you can worship with us at:
CHRIST PALACE INTERNATIONAL MINISTRIES
15152 BELLAIRE BLVD
HOUSTON, TX 77083 USA

SERVICE TIME: 10AM CST, EVERY SUNDAY.

Made in the USA
Monee, IL
10 July 2020

35469870R00042